ABOUT THE BOOK

Your feet are adapted to help you stand straight and tall. They are ready to move when you are. They help you go from where you are to where you want to be. Your feet let you follow a map through woods or city streets, make a trail over a sandy beach or hop a path over stones in a rocky brook.

You can protect your feet with shoes of many kinds. Some shoes help you use your feet in special ways. You can wear skis, snowshoes, ice skates or roller skates, or ballet slippers. As you learn sports you use waterfins, tennis shoes or football cleats.

This book tells you some of the places your feet take you. Treat them well, for they are your magic carpet to adventure.

General Editor: Margaret Farrington Bartlett

OUTDOORS ON FOOT

JIM ARNOSKY

Coward, McCann & Geoghegan, Inc. New York

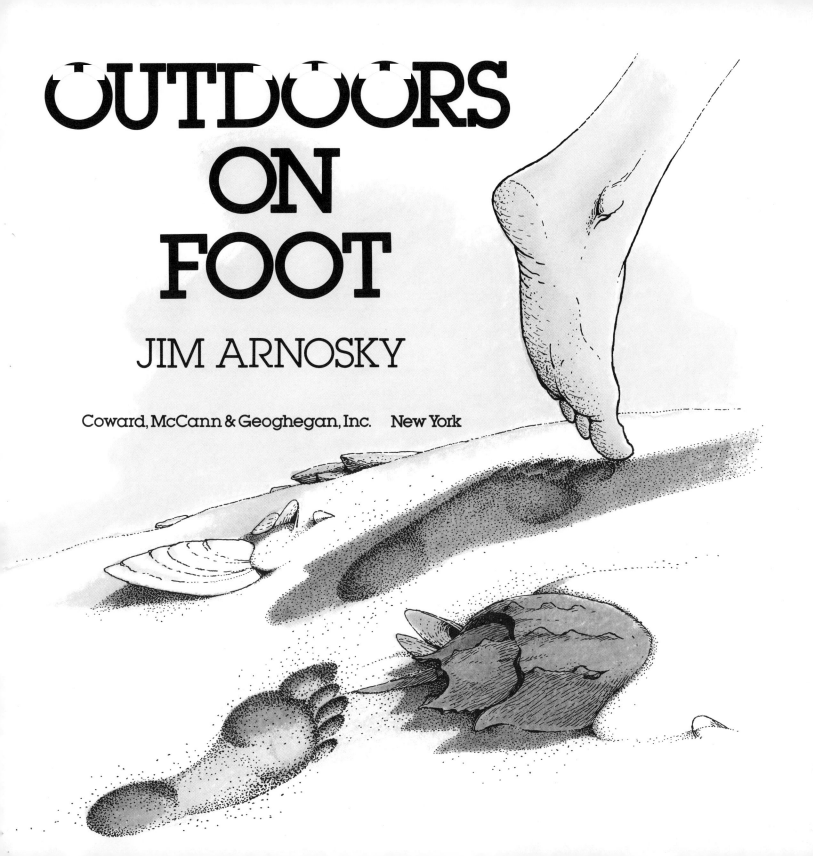

Copyright © 1978 by Jim Arnosky

All rights reserved. This book, or parts thereof, may not be reproduced in any form without permission in writing from the publishers. Published simultaneously in Canada by Longman Canada Limited, Toronto.

ISBN: 0-698-30684-8 lib. bdg.

Library of Congress Cataloging in Publication Data

Arnosky, Jim.
Outdoors on foot.
SUMMARY: Highlights the delights to be found on a nature walk.
1. Natural history—Outdoor books—Juvenile literature. 2. Walking—Juvenile literature. [1. Natural history—Outdoor books. 2. Walking] I. Title.
QH48.A73   796.5'1   77-23032

Printed in the United States of America

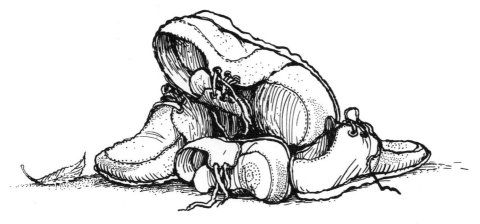

this book is dedicated to Uncle Danny

COULD YOU GROW WEBBED FEET?

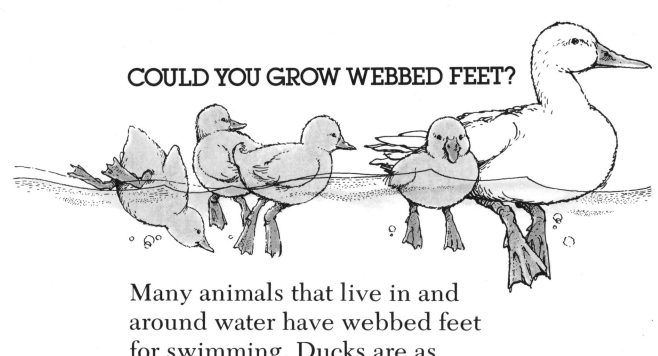

Many animals that live in and around water have webbed feet for swimming. Ducks are as comfortable in the water as they are in the air, and beavers are clumsy on land but graceful in the pond.

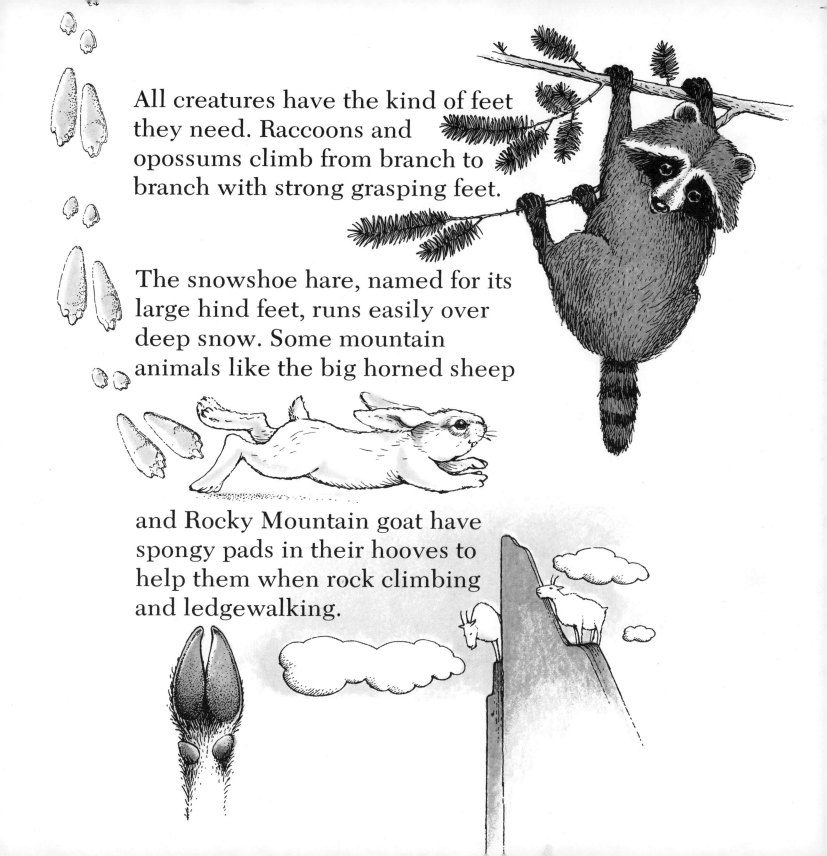

All creatures have the kind of feet they need. Raccoons and opossums climb from branch to branch with strong grasping feet.

The snowshoe hare, named for its large hind feet, runs easily over deep snow. Some mountain animals like the big horned sheep and Rocky Mountain goat have spongy pads in their hooves to help them when rock climbing and ledgewalking.

Pull your shoes and socks off and
look at your feet. You have heels
to "dig in" when going down
steep slopes. Springy arches help
to absorb the shock of hard

ground. Toes help you to stretch
up tall and peek over fences.

Your toes can fit into tiny cracks
and nooks to help you climb.
When swimming, you paddle
your feet against the water. And

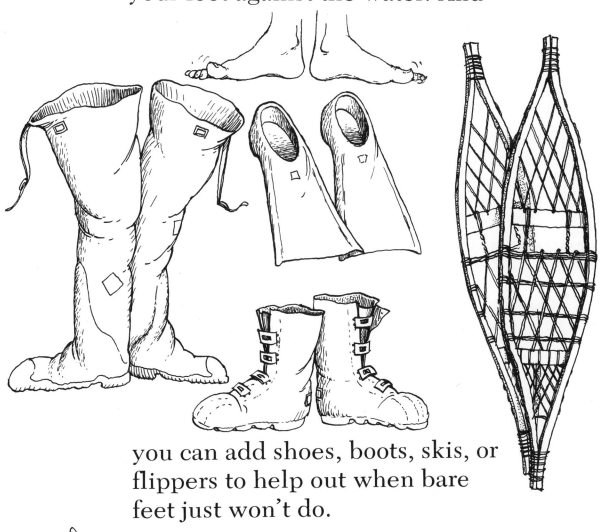

you can add shoes, boots, skis, or
flippers to help out when bare
feet just won't do.

A BAREFOOT WALK

Do you know that cool feeling
when you are walking on wet
sand and the ocean sneaks up
under your toes? Barefoot walking
is a way to really feel the world.
At the seashore you walk on hot,

dry, and loose sand. Barefoot on
cool, wet, and flat sand . . .
OUCH! Watch out for broken
shells. When you wade shin deep

in the salty water, you can close
your eyes and feel shells
tumbling over your feet and tiny
"sand crabs" burrowing in under
your step.

When you walk barefoot along a tiny stream, you press green moss or feel rounded pebbles between your toes. You climb the bank and swish through cinnamon ferns. Maybe there will be a fallen, soggy log for you to tightrope walk.

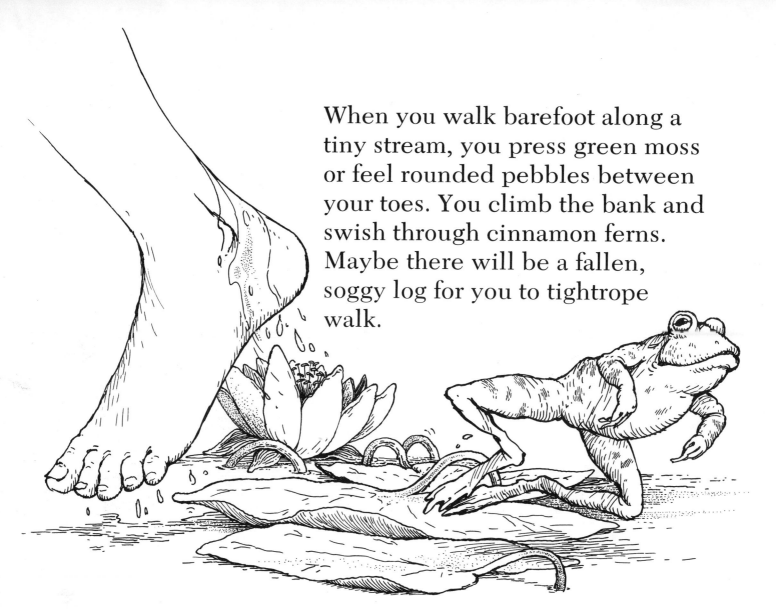

Gooey mud, firm or loose sand, can be a treat for the barefoot walker. Have you ever waded in water that felt still and warm around your legs? What color was the water? Was it weedy or filled to the brim with flat shiny lily pads? Walking through shallow moving water, you may have felt the coolness of a sparkling brook or the icy push of the river.

Do you like walking through the grass? Full-grown grass, swaying softly, is different from short, cut lawn or fragrant new-mown grass.

Tall wet grass is cool and sticks to your legs, holding you back. Dry brittle grass snaps softly under your feet . . . Watch out for stickers! Barefoot walkers find arrowheads, smooth stones and shedded snakeskins because they look carefully before stepping.

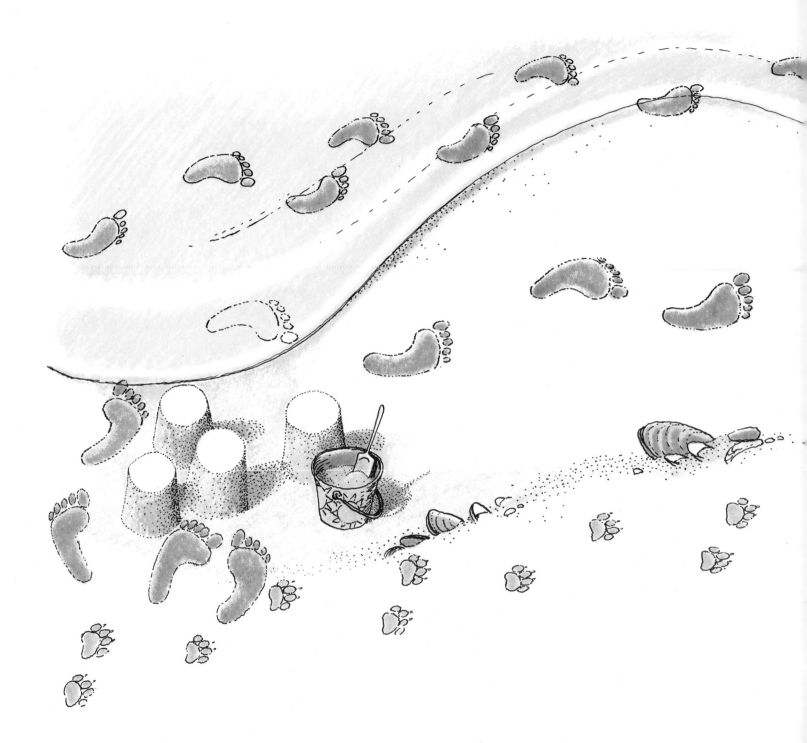

PLAYSHOES AND AUTUMN

The Indians made moccasins to
wear. You don't need moccasins,
you have your playshoes! In the
autumn, bright colored leaves
cover the ground. Leaves for
kicking, swooshing, and jumping
into.

Autumn is a special time for
wildlife. Winter approaches and
many things are happening. With
your playshoes you can follow
"rabbit runs" in and around the

hedges. Near the woods clearly marked trails may be trampled to a dark leafy mush by the constant use of deer . . . what was that snapping twig? An animal standing off the trail, watching you!

Rocky areas can be fun as long as the rocks aren't loose or slippery. Rock explorers may find hardy little trees and plants growing in crevices, or dark holes where wild animals could live.
Find a flat dry rock to sit on and watch quietly for other rock climbers, such as chipmunks, squirrels, or even a slow, wandering porcupine.

WALKING IN SNOW

In winter snow covers the land. A light covering of snow is best for making footprints and messages with your tracks.

If the snow is dry and powdery
pick up a mittenful and look at the

tiny flakes. Wet snow is for
making snowballs and forts.

North American Indians used
snowshoes to follow game over
deep snow. You too can walk over
deep snow with snowshoes!

Snowshoes are the best way to get close to wildlife because they hardly make a sound.

An animal you might like to track is yourself!

After a day of walking with your boots in the snow, can you follow your own footprints back home?

Did you stop here or turn there?
Why? You can learn a lot about
yourself from your own footprints.

Do you take long strides or short
steps? Do you jump over things or
walk around them?
Do you stop to investigate?

A WET WALK

Spring comes. The sun and warm
air melt the snow. Rain falls and
every puddle is alive.
After a spring shower walk
through the misty, rainwashed air.
Watch for birds. Their colors
seem more brilliant after a rain.

Look for earthworms on the wet
paths. Is the sky gray? Or have
the clouds blown away?
You can splash around in a
puddle left behind or watch water
flying off the toes of your boots.

When you wear waders you can explore shallow swampy areas for salamanders and frogs.
Waders are rubber boots made for walking hip or waist deep in water.

You may see a snake sliding through the water. Mosquitoes and deerflies also like to explore swamps. Ask a grown-up to explore with you!

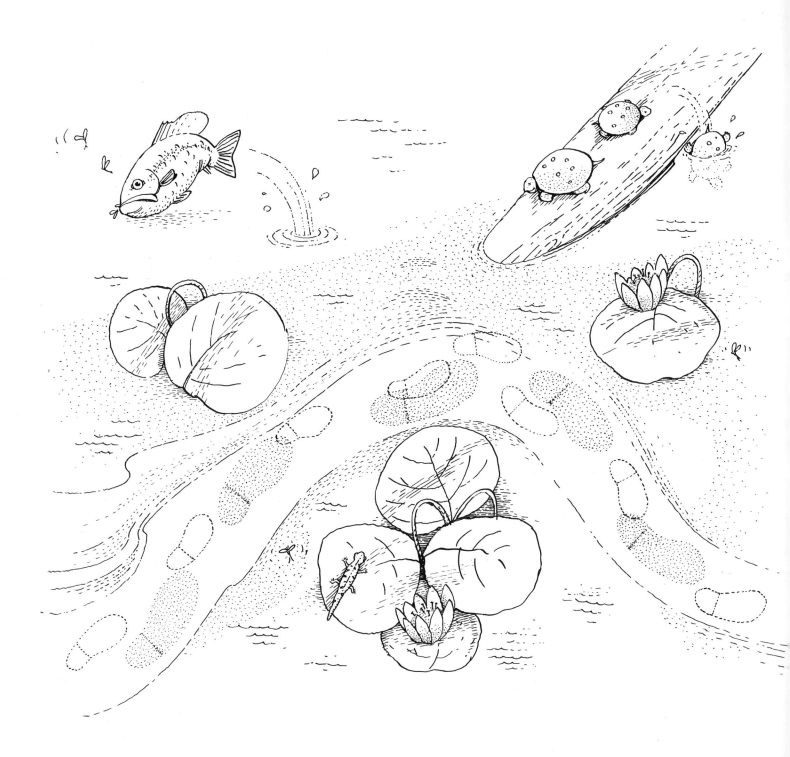

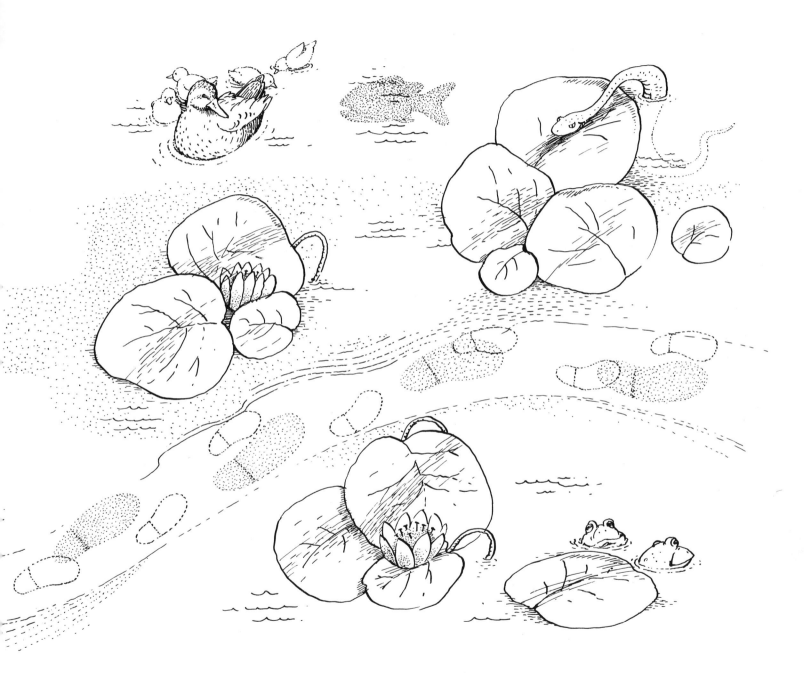

YOUR UNBEATABLE FEET

Heels, arches and toes help feet
move well in many places.
You can walk a fence, pick up
a pebble, or race with the wind.
You can climb mountains in

boots, swim oceans with flippers, and glide over ice on skates. You can explore our world and follow our seasons with every step you take.

Encourage children to discover and explore the world around them

SCIENCE AND NATURE PICTURE BOOKS

WHAT'S IN A MAP? by Sally Cartwright/illustrated by Dick Gackenbach

"This introduction to maps stresses relationships through a sensory approach to children's everyday world. Ways of making maps—with paper, blocks, sand—are included and appealing two-color line drawings enhance the text." —*School Library Journal*

"Cartwright approaches the concept of what a map is by relating the drawing of things and places to related positions in space in a way that small children can easily grasp . . . excellent introduction to the subject." —*Bulletin of the Center for Children's Books*

SUNLIGHT by Sally Cartwright/illustrated by Marylin Hafner

"This covers the sun's function as a source of light and warmth. Easy-to-read, simple experiments . . . this is a good supplement." —*School Library Journal*

". . . shows young girls and boys responding to and actively exploring sunlight throughout a day. Through her emphasis the author makes a statement missing from most of the other books, that scientific exploration is appropriate for children of both sexes." —*Appraisal*

SAND by Sally Cartwright/illustrated by Don Madden

". . . encourages observation and experimentation in a text that is sprightly, varied, and clear. The book, illustrated with lively, often humorous drawings, explains how sand is formed and what it's used for, suggests ways to investigate the properties of sand . . . and makes it all sound like great fun." —*Bulletin of the Center for Children's Books*

"Another most successful science book for the four to seven year old. . . . The text and amusing illustrations invite further exploration into the world of sand and will delight small children. . . . Recommended." —*Appraisal*

WATER IS WET by Sally Cartwright/illustrated by Marylin Hafner

"Through simple experiments and questions, this beginning science book illustrates many properties of water. The appealing blue, yellow, and green drawings, which show children doing the experiments, will stimulate first and second graders to try them." —*School Library Journal*

"A delightful way to introduce water in its many forms through simple activities which are easy and safe for young children." —*Outstanding Science Trade Books for Children in 1973— NTSTA/CBC Book Review Subcommittee*

WIND IS TO FEEL by Shirley Cook Hatch/illustrated by Marilyn Miller

". . . an excellent book . . . to encourage the child to actively investigate the world around him. We need more books such as this one to stimulate children's imaginations. All the senses are used and many simple experiments are proposed." —*AAAS Science Books*